Sayings

of a

Philosopher

John W. Friesen, Ph.D., D.Min., D.R.S.

Illustrations by David J Friesen

DETSELIG
ENTERPRISES LTD

Sayings of a Philosopher:
 © 2004 John W. Friesen, Ph.D, D.Min., D.R.S.

Library and Archives Canada Cataloguing in Publication

Friesen, John W.
 Sayings of a philosopher / John W. Friesen.

ISBN 1-55059-268-8

 1. Aphorisms and apothegms. I. Title.

PS8561.R4958S29 2004   C818'.5402   C2004-904430-3

Detselig Enterprises Ltd.
210, 1220 Kensington Road NW
Calgary, Alberta T2N 3P5

Phone: (403) 283-0900
Fax: (403) 283-6947
Email: temeron@telusplanet.net
www.temerondetselig.com

We acknowledge the support of the Government of Canada through the
Book Publishing Industry Development Program (BPIDP) for our publishing program.

We also acknowledge the support of the Alberta Foundation for the Arts
for our publishing program.

Alberta Foundation for the Arts   Alberta COMMUNITY DEVELOPMENT
COMMITTED TO THE DEVELOPMENT OF CULTURE AND THE ARTS

SAN 113-0234
Printed in Canada

INTRODUCTION

This little volume is made up of a series of reflections on a variety of subjects derived from a myriad of sources. Not unlike informal "pontifical" musings, these thoughts were collected over several decades while involved in the business of teaching philosophy, doing pastoral work, counselling, and preaching.

It has often been said that people tend to take life too seriously; some of the thoughts in this book will hopefully change that perspective. Taking a slightly lighter approach to the vicissitudes of everyday life can be quite healthy.

In some instances these sayings reflect the Canadian fondness for clever remarks. Beware, however, because a few serious proposals are also included!

Americans may prefer put-down humor and the British their puns. This made-up collection is purely Canadian.

Enjoy!

J.W.F.

To my brother Don, the Minister,

who is always in need of pithy sayings.

CONTENTS

MARRIAGE AND FAMILY

Partner Selection

It is always good advice to select a marriage partner with the same faith as you have. If you have no faith, find someone who also believes in nothing. It may not be much, but at least that way you will have *something* in common.

Never marry someone who hasn't been in love before and who hasn't been dumped by somebody. If your future partner isn't familiar with both of these experiences, he or she will probably wonder about them during all the years of your marriage.

Let them get over it first.

Choosing a Name

Married couples should initially choose a name to describe their marital bliss and amend it every five years.

Initially, the couple could take the name,

"Mr. & Ms. Joyous," or
Mr. & Ms. "Happy-for-Eternity."

Five years later;
"Mr. & Ms. Mistake," or "Mr. & Ms. Regrets."

Ten years;

"Mr. & Ms. Deadbeat," or

"Mr. & Ms. Struggling."

Twenty-five years;

"Mr. & Ms. Hadit," or "Mr. & Ms. Resigned."

Related fact:

43 percent of all weddings are second marriages
for at least one individual involved.

More on Names

A newlywed couple might want to choose a name together, perhaps by combining their names.

Jack Badsinc and Mary Lipbratt could become "Mr. And Ms. Lipsinc," or Mr. & Ms. "Badbrat."

Joe Uratt and Susan Thog could become "Mr. & Ms. Urahog."

Charlie Chugant and Joanne Balug could become "Mr. & Mrs. Chugalug."

On I.Q.

A recent study found that each successive child a couple has will have an IQ three points lower than the previous one. Perhaps having only one child might be a wise choice.

Related Thought: Research may have got it wrong. The first child should be considered a prototype, and the second one the "real thing." The intelligence of successive children will probably deteriorate.

The fact that I'm a second child should in no way affect the objectivity of this statement. My wife agrees with me; oops, she's a second child too!

Heredity

If your parents didn't have any children, there's a good chance you won't have any either!

The problem with the family gene pool
is that there is no lifeguard.

Death, by the way, is also hereditary.

On Daycares

The recent surge in traffic in larger urban centres has raised fears about safety in dropping off children at local daycare centres.

It might alleviate fears somewhat if the daycare centre administration would consider building a chute on the roadway adjacent to the daycare.

That way children could slide to safety while enjoying the ride.

RELIGION

Heaven

Heaven is a place where you have no assignments or obligations, and you still don't feel bored.

Garden of Eden

There probably never was a Garden of Eden. The concept of such a garden is really a metaphor about teenagers rebelling against their parents.

We should have seen it coming!

When the Bible says that God punished Adam and Eve by chasing them out of the Garden of Eden, the story is really a metaphor for God saying, "From now on you will have children!"

Definition of Hell

When control freaks die, God lets them con-
sciously view what their family and friends are
doing on the earth and they can't do anything
about it.

On Wisdom

It has been suggested that King Solomon was a very wise man.

Obviously he was.

Look how many advisors he had in the form of his 1 000 wives and concubines!

SOCIAL-POLITICAL PROBLEMS

Age Discrimination

One way to handle the problem of age discrimination would be to start a firm and hire *only* people over 65 years of age.

Modern Apparel

Today's Mother Hubbard, goes to the cupboard,
To get her poor daughter a dress,
And when she gets there, the cupboard is bare,
But so is her daughter, I guess!

Cutting the Cost of Smoking

One way to speed up a busy smoker's schedule and cut costs at the same time would be to set up a room with a continual nicotine blast so smokers' needs can be more efficiently met. A few minutes in such a room could expedite matters much more quickly than the traditional method of smoking.

If the nicotine yearn is based on oral tendencies, smoker's could be provided with a pacifier to aid in inhaling.

Related fact: When a certain lecturer concluded his talk and it was time for the question period, he always took questions from smokers first because he knew they didn't have as much time.

On Housing

City planners and construction companies seem to have a penchant for building little toy houses (known as starter homes), that all look alike and are located four feet (just over a metre) apart.

An alternate solution would simply be to build row housing. This arrangement would require that less walls be built, and result in considerable savings in heat bills. It would also eliminate rows and rows of silly little narrow houses.

Hopefully, people will eventually get over the idea that a house has to have four independent sides in order for resident "warriors" to be able to properly "protect their castles." Perhaps an interim form of therapy for both builders and buyers would be an appropriate measure.

Preserving Public Lawns

Public lawns could better be preserved if temporary sidewalks were first built in order to determine where people actually walk. Once this has been established, permanent sidewalks can be installed.

Alternately, it might be a good idea to build sidewalks that represent the shortest distance between two points.

Government Procedures

Whenever a social issue arises, instead of doing something about it, governments usually form a committee or government commission to provide a label for the phenomenon.

They give the commission several years to investigate and by the time the commission completes their work, new issues have risen and everyone has forgotten about the old problem.

Using this approach, the government doesn't have to do anything about the original problem.

Eliminating Prostitution

This not a good idea.

Human nature being what it is, it would be impossible to eliminate it anyway.

Eliminating or regulating prostitution could cause a severe disruption in the nation's social system.

Legalizing prostitution, for example, would probably make the practice socially acceptable. What would this do for the thousands of married politicians, professionals, businessmen, and celebrities, who like to "live on the edge" in terms of marital infidelity and the risk of contracting biologically transmittable diseases?

Eliminating Strikes

A quick and effective approach would be to take three company managers and three union workers, put them into a hotel room, and feed them nothing but fast-food until they come to a resolution.

It should take no longer than three days!

On Pollution

If politicians were really serious about pollution, they would give a $5 000 tax break to everyone who moves close enough to their place of work so they can walk to work.

Such a move would severely cut back on gas consumption and greatly reduce smog.

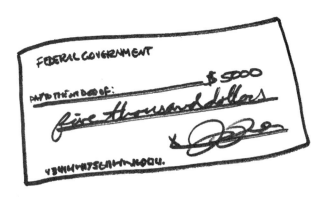

Imagine the financial spin-off value of such a move. The economy would surge because everyone would have more money from not having to drive to work Also, many people from a variety of professions would make a great deal of money – movers, builders, installers, electricians, plumbers, etc. People saving money by this arrangement would pump their extra cash right back into the economy, by buying bigger Christmas presents. Everyone would win.

Estimated value of the new government policy to the economy would be 55 billion dollars annually.

How did I arrive at this figure?

The same way government bureaucrats do when they prepare budgets.

I made it up!

On Multiculturalism

A serious approach to reducing prejudice, racism, and discrimination, would be to give a $5 000 tax break to anyone who marries someone from a religion, creed, culture, or race different from their own.

Imagine the financial spin-off value of such a policy (See previous page)!

SPORTS AND HOBBIES

Golf

No rational person can possibly understand the logic of golf.

It seems that golfers like to carry expensive little white balls with them which they hit into swamps, creeks, or bushes and then go look for them.

If the little white balls are so precious, why not put them into a display case in the den and admire them?

Apparently people engage in golf for exercise. If exercise is so important, why not just go for a walk and keep those expensive little white balls?

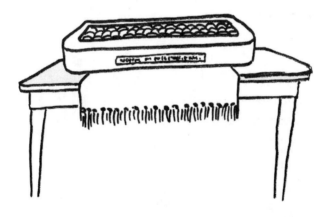

Better Armies

Canada's solution to building a better army is really quite simple.

Military trainees should be taught to play Canadian hockey.

Canadian hockey teams have some of the best fighters in the world.

Interestingly, when hockey players fight on ice they are called hockey players, when they should be called warriors.

By contrast, when military trainees put on a uniform they are called peacekeepers.

Something's not working here!

Football

Some years ago, Thomas Hornsby Ferrill described football as a ceremony consisting of opposing groups of young male priests attempting to carry the egg of life (a ball of inflated pigskin) across four lines representing the four seasons.

The ceremony is celebrated at halftime with boisterous music accompanying the dance of the semi-nude virgins (sometimes called cheerleaders). When one of the priests carries the egg of life across a seasonal line, the kneeling virgins bury their faces in the ground and raise their arms to heaven in supplication.

That about sums it up.
Football is probably just another form of religion!

Quilting

Come to think of it, the art of quilting is a little like the self-defeating game of golf.

Why would anyone take a perfectly good piece of fabric, cut it into little pieces, and then sew them back together to make a quilt?

Why not use that nice piece of fabric as a bed cover in the first place?

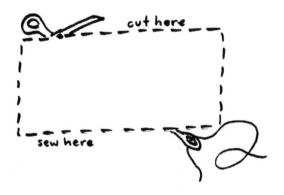

PERSONAL

Discovering One's Self

There are four ways in which this can be accomplished:

a)Simply look at your birth certificate, the picture on your driver's license, or your library card.

That's who you are!

b)Take a good hard look at your parents; you will undoubtedly turn out like one of them anyway.

c)Look in any mirror.

d)Better still, ask your spouse or neighbor who you are; they will tell you pretty quickly!

Being Realistic

When someone says, "Let's be realistic," they simply mean, "Let's do it my way!"

Showing Off

Showing off is an idiot's interpretation of being interesting.

Avoiding Trouble

Be very careful, and nothing good or bad will *ever* happen to you.

End of Life

After a certain age, if you don't wake up aching in every joint, you are probably dead.

Overweight

A good way to camouflage a weight problem is to change friends. Begin to hang around with heavier people; that way *you* will appear lighter.

Dealing with Change

This is kind of complicated because people tend to react in different ways.

First, there are people who get all excited about change and then let their enthusiasm fizzle within 24 hours,

Second, there are people who try to make it *look like* they are accepting change; and,

Third, there are people who wait to see if anybody else is making change so they can follow suit.

Approaches to Change

Some people make things happen, some people watch things happen, and others say, "what happened?"

" HUH?"

Success

If at first you don't succeed,
destroy all the evidence that you even tried.

On Memory

Practice calling your mate by different names so that when you do lose your memory, no one will know.

Parents do this all the time, often pretending they can't keep the names of their children straight.

It is a little difficult to pull this off if you only have one child.

On Looks

It has been said that beauty is only skin deep, but ugliness of character goes right to the bone.

NATIONAL AND
INTERNATIONAL RELATIONS

Canadian Climate

Immigrants from Siberia smile even during Canadian winters because they are glad they are not still in Siberia where the winters are even harsher.

Canadian Seasons

(i)   Dreading winter;

(ii)   Preparing for winter;

(iii) Enduring winter; and,

(iv)   Recovering from winter.

Successful Marketing

The underlying strategy is to get more people to buy more things more often for more money.

SALE   SALE   SALE

Statistics Canada

Canada owns 15 percent of the world's 595 816 kilometres (372 385 miles) of the world's coast-line.

That may not mean much to you, but there must be *someone* out there who cares about this.

HARDCORE PHILOSOPHY

The Irish philosopher, George Berkeley, once asked, "If a tree falls in a forest and there is no one around to hear it fall, does it make a noise?"

The answer, of course is, "no," because the tree in question was probably deaf.

This statement may not make sense at first, but debates such as this built the field of philosophy.

As someone once said, "defining philosophy is like a blind man going into a dark room looking for a black cat that isn't there!"

Here are a few definitions that keep philosophers active.

Ontology

Ontology is the study of what is *really* real. Of course no one really knows what is real, but the pursuit affords a lifetime career for philosophers who are not otherwise employable.

Metaphysics

Metaphysics is an attempt to explain the real nature of the universe, not that anyone knows what the *unreal* nature of the universe might be.

Epistemology

Epistemology is the study of truth as opposed to the study of lies.

Simple as it may sound, the search has been going on since the time of Adam and Eve. Was Adam seduced or did he con Eve into getting his breakfast for him? Was it really an apple, an orange, or a bunch of grapes she was offering?

No one knows for sure.

Axiology

Axiology is actually the study of axes. Some-where along the line someone stuck in the suffix "ology" to make it sound more mysterious.

A more sophisticated answer is that axiology is the study of what is valuable or worthwhile.

Oops, that was a bit serious!

Settling a question of axiology would depend on one's culture, mood, taste, time, or place – maybe even height and weight or the time of day. It is *that* vague!

Ethics and Aesthetics

Ethics deals with . . .

what constitutes acceptable behavior (keep in mind that nowadays anything goes); or,

how one should behave when others are watching.

Aesthetics is the study of . . .

who or what is beautiful or artistically pleasing (try to keep Hollywood out of this); or,

things that can readily be marketed as "nice things."

Idealism

Idealism is actually the study of ideas. The letter "L" was stuck in for literary ease somewhere along the line.

Idealism has *nothing* to do with ideals,
much like today's way of thinking and acting.

Existentialism

Supposedly existentialism is the view that people exist in a purposeless world, but selfism has changed the meaning of the term.

Today the purpose of life is to make oneself happy even if just for the moment or at the expense of others.

Thomism

Thomism is supposed to be the belief system of Thomas Aquinas, and was once called "Aquini-anistic thought." Since no one could pronounce or spell the word this form of philosophy eventually became known as *Thomism*.

By bringing up Aquinas's thought in modern times we get to call it *Neo-Thomism*.

Nowadays it would probably be called . . .

Postmodern NeoThomism.

Postmodernism

Postmodernism is a currently much-touted belief system that holds three positions:

(i) There is no reality, only individual perception;

(ii) Everyone is entitled to full privilege of interpretation,
without having to take responsibility for it;

and,

(iii) Everyone's opinion is equally valid regardless of age or experience, role or rank, education or training. After all, "we're all equal here!"

Fifty years ago it was called "nihilism," which is a denial of the existence of any basis for knowledge or truth.

The question is, "where do we go from here?"

Pragmatism

The dictionary suggests that pragmatism is the belief system that tests the validity of any claim.

In real life it is the view that you can justify anything you do but you don't have to.

Relief

Aren't you glad you don't have to teach philosophy?

SCIENCE AND
MISCELLANEOUS

Computers or Elephants?

Both elephants and computers store information; that is, they "remember things." However, computers are better.

Can you imagine taking an elephant on a plane instead of a laptop? Computers are smaller, require less feeding, and are easier to handle.

More on Elephants

Asian elephants are the only animals (besides humans) that can stand on their heads!

That fact has got to mean *something* to *someone*.

On Dogs

Everyone should have a dog because dogs are friendly. It has been proven that people tend to take on the characteristics of those they hang around with.

Imagine, if everyone had a dog they would go around wagging their tails, trying to lather up someone's leg, and be very happy.

Most likely, no one would go to work.

That wouldn't be so bad would it?

On Gift Horses

Never look a gift horse in the mouth; most horses have very bad breath!

On Mosquitoes

It has been reported that 1.2 million mosquitoes simultaneously biting an individual could drain that person's blood supply.

Luckily, mosquitoes aren't that organized.

Grading Chickens

Chickens should be graded on the same scale as anyone else.

Simply have each chicken write an essay on a specific topic, and assign evaluators to read the essays.

Swimsuits

The historical record has it that the United States government should be thanked for the origin of the bikini. As part of wartime rationing, in 1943 the US government ordered a 10 percent reduction in the use of fabric for women's swimwear.

Apparently that started a trend.

Four Food groups for the Twenty-first Century

Microwave, non-microwave, junkfood, and chocolate;

Or,

French fries, gravy, potato chips, and soda pop.

Music ♪

One of the latest country songs pretty well sums up the signs of the times:

"If You Don't Leave Me Alone,
I'll Go and Find Someone Else Who Will."

Preserving the Human Brain

For mad scientists who keep brains in jars, adding a slice of lemon to each jar could help preserve the brain.

Alternately, one could simply keep playing mind-numbing video games.

Love

My parents, Gerhard and Barbara Friesen, were married for 67 years. One day when my father was helping my mother put on her coat, an observer remarked to her, "Oh, second husband, eh? He seems so attentive."

"Oh no," My mother replied, "He's been doing this for 67 years!"

ABOUT THE AUTHOR

John W. Friesen, Ph.D., D.Min., D.R.S, a native of Saskatchewan, holds a doctorate in philosophy of education from the University of Kansas and is a Professor in the Graduate Division of Educational Research at the University of Calgary. He is an ordained minister with the All Native Circle Conference of the United Church of Canada.

Although the academic calibre of his "wise" sayings might not reflect it, he also graduated from six other colleges including Bethany College, Concord College, Tabor College, Emporia State University, Christian Bible College, and Trinity Theological Seminary.

Other of his books published by Temeron/Detselig include:

People, Culture and Learning, 1977;

Strangled Roots, 1982;

Schools With A Purpose, 1983;

When Cultures Clash: Case Studies in Multiculturalism, 1985, 1993;

The Cultural Maze: Complex Questions on Native Destiny in Western Canada, 1991;

Pick One: A User Friendly Guide to Religion, 1995;

Rediscovering the First Nations of Canada, 1997;

Sayings of the Elders: An Anthology of First Nations Wisdom, 1998;

First Nations of the Plains: Creative, Adaptable, and Enduring, 1999;

Legends of the Elders, 2000;

Aboriginal Spirituality and Biblical Theology: Closer Than You Think, 2000;

In Defense of Public Schools in North America, (co-author), 2001;

Aboriginal Education in Canada: A Plea for Integration, (co-author), 2002;

More Legends of the Elders, (co-author), 2004; and,

We Are Included: The Métis People of Canada Realize Riel's Vision, (co-author), 2004.